ANCIENT MYTHOLOGY

JAPANESE MYTHS AND LEGENDS

by Janie Havemeyer
illustrated by Cesar Samaniego

Tools for Parents & Teachers

Grasshopper Books enhance imagination and introduce the earliest readers to fun storylines and illustrations. The easy-to-read text supports early reading experiences with repetitive sentence patterns and sight words.

Before Reading
- Discuss the cover illustration. What do readers see?
- Look at the glossary together. Discuss the words.

During Reading
- "Walk" through the book with the reader. Discuss new or unfamiliar words. Sound them out together.
- Look at the illustrations. When and where does the story take place? What is happening in the story?

After Reading
- Prompt the child to think more. Ask: What is your favorite Japanese legend? Why?

Grasshopper Books are published by Jump!
3500 American Blvd W, Suite 150
Bloomington, MN 55431
www.jumplibrary.com

Copyright © 2026 Jump! International copyright reserved in all countries. No part of this book may be reproduced in any form without written permission from the publisher.

Jump! is a division of FlutterBee Education Group.

Library of Congress Cataloging-in-Publication Data

Names: Havemeyer, Janie, author.
Samaniego, César, 1975- illustrator.
Title: Japanese myths and legends / by Janie Havemeyer; Illustrated by Cesar Samaniego.
Description: Minneapolis, MN: Jump!, Inc., [2026]
Series: Ancient mythology | Includes index.
Audience: Ages 7-10
Identifiers: LCCN 2024054444 (print)
LCCN 2024054445 (ebook)
ISBN 9798892137539 (hardcover)
ISBN 9798892137546 (paperback)
ISBN 9798892137553 (ebook)
Subjects: LCSH: Mythology, Japanese–Juvenile literature.
Gods, Japanese–Folklore–Juvenile literature.
Goddesses, Japanese–Folklore–Juvenile literature.
Classification: LCC BL2203 .H42 2026 (print)
LCC BL2203 (ebook)
DDC 398.20952–dc23/eng/20250110
LC record available at https://lccn.loc.gov/2024054444
LC ebook record available at https://lccn.loc.gov/2024054445

Editor: Alyssa Sorenson
Direction and Layout: Anna Peterson
Illustrator: Cesar Samaniego
Content Consultant: Gustav Heldt, PhD, Professor of Japanese Literature, University of Virginia

Printed in the United States of America at Corporate Graphics in North Mankato, Minnesota.

Table of Contents

Sun, Sea, and Storms 4
Japanese Gods and Goddesses 22
To Learn More 23
Glossary 24
Index 24

Sun, Sea, and Storms

The **creator** gods Izanami and Izanagi stood on a cloud bridge between heaven and Earth. The ocean was beneath them. There was no land to stand on.

They stirred the ocean with a spear. Water droplets fell from it. They hardened. They turned into the first Japanese island!

Japanese people have told **legends** of gods, goddesses, and heroes for more than 1,000 years. Gods have magical powers. They can help or hurt people.

Kagutsuchi is the Japanese god of fire. People give **offerings** to make him happy. They hope his flames will not burn their towns.

Amaterasu is the Sun goddess. She brings sunlight to Earth. Her brother is Susa-no-o. He is the storm god. He stirs up trouble.

Once, Amaterasu planted beautiful rice fields in heaven. Susa-no-o let horses run through. They wrecked the fields.

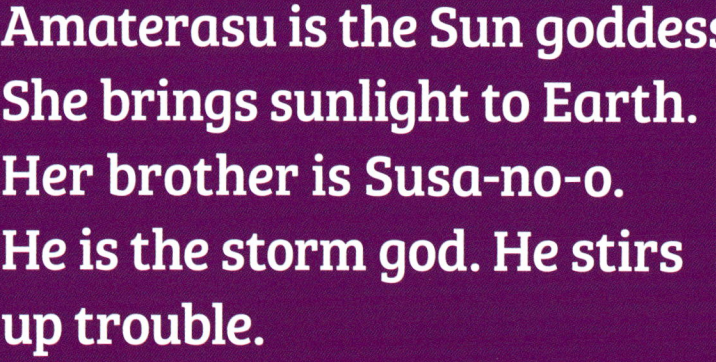

Another time, Susa-no-o cut a hole in Amaterasu's roof. He threw a horse at her! Amaterasu left heaven to get away from him.

Ame-no-Uzume is the goddess of dawn. She is known for dancing and being funny. She wanted Amaterasu to come home. She danced outside her cave. Other gods laughed and cheered her on. Amaterasu came out to see. She returned light to the world.

There was a time when day and night were not separate. Tsuki-yomi, the Moon god, lived in heaven with Amaterasu. The Moon and Sun shone together in the sky.

One day, Tsuki-yomi and Amaterasu had a fight. Tsuki-yomi went to the other side of the world. Now, Tsuki-yomi appears at night. Amaterasu lights the world during the day.

Every night, a monster attacked the **emperor**'s palace. Yorimasa was a human **warrior**. He was the only person brave enough to face the monster.

He hid outside the palace. At midnight, the monster landed on the roof. Yorimasa aimed his bow and arrow. He shot the monster. He saved the emperor! Yorimasa became a hero.

Fujin and Raijin are twins. They are weather gods. One day, they saw ships sailing to Japan. Warriors were coming to **invade**!

Raijin beat his thunder drums. He threw lightning bolts. Fujin used his bag of air to create wind. The brothers did this for two days. They destroyed the enemy's ships. They saved Japan.

Gods still protect Japan. People visit **shrines**. They ring a bell to greet the gods. They bow. They pray and thank the gods!

Japanese Gods and Goddesses

Who are the most important Japanese gods and goddesses? Take a look!

Amaterasu
Sun goddess

Ame-no-Uzume
Goddess of dawn

Ebisu
God of luck, success, and fishermen

Fujin
Wind god

Izanagi and Izanami
Creator gods

Kagutsuchi
God of fire

Raijin
God of thunder

Susa-no-o
Storm god

Tsuki-yomi
Moon god

To Learn More

Finding more information is as easy as 1, 2, 3.

❶ Go to www.factsurfer.com
❷ Enter "**Japanesemythsandlegends**" into the search box.
❸ Choose your book to see a list of websites.

Glossary

creator: A person who creates, or makes, something.
emperor: A male ruler of an empire.
invade: To enter by force in order to take over.
legends: Stories handed down from earlier times.
offerings: Gifts given to gods.
shrines: Buildings or small structures people visit to worship gods.
warrior: A person who fights in a battle or war.

Index

Amaterasu 8, 10, 11, 12, 14
Ame-no-Uzume 12
cloud bridge 4
emperor 16
Fujin 18, 19
heaven 4, 8, 10, 14
island 5
Izanagi 4, 5
Izanami 4, 5
Kagutsuchi 6
offerings 6
Raijin 18, 19
ships 18, 19
shrines 20
Susa-no-o 8, 10
Tsuki-yomi 14
warrior 16, 18
Yorimasa 16